A Dog's Christmas on the Beach

A Dog's Christmas on the Beach

Sarah Fischer Pointer

This book is dedicated to all the Maltese dogs out there and the families that love them. Also dedicated to the shelter and rescue employees and volunteers, along with the veterinarians, that keep them healthy and safe.

In memory of my dear Casper, who passed away at age of 15, and my little boy Q- Tip, who is also getting up there in years but will always be deeply loved.

A house is not a home without a Maltese!

There once was a Maltese dog that LOVED Christmas. He loved the garland hanging over the living room picture window, and the big fir tree with all the lights, tinsel and ornaments on it. He loved the big lighted star that Daddy always put on top of the tree when Mommy and Sissy were done decorating it, and he loved the short, chubby dancing Santa in his red coat and black boots that Mommy always put by the front door.

He even loved the snow that would fall in big white flakes and always hoped there would be lots of it left on the ground for him to play in. Whenever it snowed for the first time, the dog and his sister would go outside and build a snowman. They would get all bundled up and Sissy would roll three big balls of snow together, put them one on top of the other, and would add coal and carrots for the snowman's eyes and nose, and sticks for his arms.

The dog's favorite part of Christmas was Christmas Eve, when Mommy, Daddy and Sissy would take him with them on a ride all around town to look at the Christmas decorations. They would see all the houses in their neighborhood, looking so bright and cheery. There would be lots of Christmas trees in the neighbors' windows, all lit up, and lots of lights on their porches and roofs. The dog would stick his head out the window and bark at all the blow up Santas and snowmen.

But this year for Christmas, Mommy said they were all going somewhere called Florida to see Grandma and Grandpa Werner. The dog was excited to see Grandma and Grandpa again, but he was nervous because this would be his first long car ride, and he'd never been away from home for the holidays.

Sissy had been to Florida before and she told the dog all about the warm weather and the beautiful beaches, but the dog was afraid that Christmas just wouldn't be the same if he wasn't at home for it. What if they didn't have all the pretty decorations in Florida that they had in Illinois? What if there was no snow? What if Santa couldn't find them at Grandma and Grandpa's house?!

One week before Christmas, Mommy and Daddy packed up the car with all their luggage. Sissy brought lots of books to read and some movies to watch on her tablet and she even brought the dog's bed and his favorite toys to keep them entertained on the way. Sissy and the dog hopped in the back seat, and Daddy started driving.

They drove, and they drove, and they drove. They drove through little towns covered in snow. They drove down mountain roads where you could see over the edge to the bottom far below. They drove all day long, and when it got dark out, they stopped for the night.

After breakfast and a quick walk, they all got back in the car. They drove, and they drove, and they drove some more. It was getting so warm out now that they could roll the car windows down! The dog took his sweater off, stuck his head out the window, and sniffed at the warm air. He could smell water.

They stopped at a rest stop for lunch, and everyone changed into shorts. They all got back in the car and drove a little further. "Almost there," Daddy said as they left the highway. "We'll be at Grandma and Grandpa's in no time!"

Daddy turned right into a mobile home park and a few minutes later he pulled into Grandma and Grandpa's driveway. Grandma and Grandpa Werner came out of the house, smiling and saying, "You're here!" Sissy jumped out of the car and ran to hug them, while the dog stepped out of the car nervously.

He recognized Grandma and Grandpa from their house up north, and was happy to see them again, but Florida sure was a strange place! The grass, the trees, and even the homes looked and smelled so different than the ones back in Illinois. Once they'd gotten their luggage out of the car and put it in the guest room, Sissy decided to take the dog on a walk.

After walking a few blocks, the dog saw something white and fluffy on the ground ahead. *Oh, boy, snow*! He thought. He pulled Sissy along and jumped into it. But wait, this wasn't snow! It was warm, soft and heavy, instead of cold and fluffy. He looked at Sissy, confused.

"Isn't the sand nice?" Sissy asked, sitting down on it and lifting her face to the sun. The dog sniffed around a little. He guessed the sand wsa nice, but it just wasn't the same as snow! It wouldn't really be like Christmas without snow.

While walking along the beach, the dog saw a strange little tree with some lights on it. They were Christmas lights! Maybe it would be more like Christmas here than the dog thought. He went over to the tree and sniffed it.

This wasn't a spruce tree like back home, it was too short and spiny. And the only leaves on it were some long green leaves sticking out of the top. "Isn't this palm tree pretty?! I palm trees with Christmas lights on them," Sissy said. The lights were nice, the dog thought, but a palm tree just wasn't the same. It wouldn't really be like Christmas without his spruce tree!

Sissy and the dog walked back to Grandma and Grandpa's house and played Candy Land with them for a while. Then, Daddy suggested they all go looking at Christmas lights. *Oh, boy*, the dog thought, *now this will be like Christmas back home*!

They all piled into Grandma and Grandpa's van and drove along the shore. There were so many lights! Lots of the houses had Christmas trees in their windows, and lights put up along their roofs and on the railings of their front porches. And a lot of them even had blow up decorations in their yards, just like at home!

18

But what was this? Instead of Santa Clause, these blow up decorations looked like alligators and flamingos with Santa hats on! And there were palm trees with little ball ornaments and lights on them. *Silly people*, thought the dog, *alligators and flamingoes aren't for Christmas*!

The next day, the whole family spent the afternoon at the beach. Sissy and the dog splashed around in the water and ran up and down the beach while the grown-ups sat in the shade.

"Look at that!" Sissy shouted, pointing out into the water. The dog looked and he saw a man dressed like Santa. *Oh, boy, Santa*! He thought. But... this Santa was too young and skinny to be the real Santa. He was wearing shorts, and was standing on a wooden board, riding it through the water!

"It's a surfing Santa!" Sissy laughed. *What silly things these people in Florida do*, the dog thought. *Don't they know Santa is old and chubby, and he definitely can't surf!*

22

The next day was Christmas Eve. The dog was feeling a little sad, thinking about how different things were down here in Florida. Alligators with Santa hats. A surfing Santa. It just wasn't like Christmas without things they way they were back home!

Grandma, Mommy and Sissy got an artificial Christmas tree out of the garage and started to put it up. They put up little ornaments, and strung lights around the tree. And then Grandpa put a big angel at the top of the tree. It was so pretty!

That night, they all went to a Christmas Eve church service on the beach. While it was strange being on the beach for church, the dog loved the manger scene that they had set up and hearing all the old songs that they used to sing back home for Christmas.

Before bed, Grandma, Mommy and Sissy baked some cookies for Santa. They were chocolate chip cookies and they smelled so good! But the dog couldn't have any. Sissy put the cookies on a plate with a cup of milk and a little note for Santa before they went to bed.

The next morning, the dog found presents under the tree! Santa had found them, even in Florida. Grandma and Grandpa got homemade Christmas ornaments that Sissy had made them. Sissy got some new books, and a new doll. Mommy got a pretty Christmas sweater, and Daddy got some new golf gloves. And the dog got a new bone! It was delicious.

After the presents were opened, Grandma made a big dinner for them. There was ham and turkey and sweet potatoes, with dressing and green bean casserole and pumpkin pie. Sissy even snuck pieces of ham and turkey to the dog under the table when no one was looking.

As everyone ate their dessert, the dog looked around at his happy family and his heart was full of love. He realized that the most important part of Christmas wasn't the decorations, the weather, or the trees. It was family! And the best part of Christmas was being with the people he loved most.

Sarah Fischer Pointer is an attorney and author living in Southwest Florida. In her spare time, she enjoys reading, writing, and spending time with her own little Maltese dog, especially around the holidays!